Published By Robert Corbin

@ Brian Hubler

Low-fodmap Diet Cookbook: Your Low-carb, High-fat to Easy and Delicious Low-sodium and Low-potassium Recipes

All Right RESERVED

ISBN 978-87-94477-13-0

TABLE OF CONTENTS

Kid Friendly Low Fodmap Cookbook 1

Low Fodmap Spaghetti Bolognese: 3

Grilled Salmon With Lemon: 5

Low Fodmap Chicken Fried Rice: 6

Tortilla Baked Eggs 8

Asian Chicken Salad 11

Whole Roast Chicken & Vegetables 14

Bacon And Brie Frittata 17

Baked Eggs And Ham Cups (4 Servings) 19

Hash Browns 21

Breakfast Sausage 23

Breakfast & Brunch 24

Cheese, Ham, And Spinach Muffins 24

Crunchy Granola 26

Crepes And Berries 28

Chapter Three 30

Chocolate Pancakes 30

Cornbread Muffins 33

Green Kiwi Smoothie.. 36

Low Fodmap Recipes.. 38

  Greek-Style Roasted Chicken With Lemon And Oregano 38

Grilled Chicken With Roasted Vegetables: 41

Low Fodmap Buffalo Chicken Dip 43

Low Fodmap Antipasto Skewers 45

Lemon Parsley Roasted Shrimp.. 46

Parmesan Roasted Broccoli... 48

Orange Cranberry Walnut Scones 50

Dry Belly Soup With Cabbage And Celery 53

Dry Soup Recipe For Pumpkin Belly 55

Cornbread Waffles 57

Low Fodmap Breakfast Pork Sausage Patties................. 60

Cheesy Frittata 63

Sweet And Savory Corn Bread.. 65

Low Fodmap Mini Pizzas: 68

- Low Fodmap Turkey Tacos: 69
- Low Fodmap Veggie Stir-Fry: 71
- Low Fodmap Chicken And Rice Soup: 73
- Berry Nice Muesli 75
- Macaroni Slaw 77
- Reakfast Burrito 80
- Potatoes 82
- Breakfast Quesadilla 83
- Cheesy Corn Muffins 84
- Crispy Rice Balls With Parmesan And Corn 87
- Vegetable Curry With quinoa 89
- Chocolate Avocado Waffles 92
- Diy Low Fodmap & Gluten Free Waffle Mix 94
- Gluten Free Egg And Cheese Soufflé 96
- Dry Belly Soup Recipe With Cabbage 98
- Dry Belly Soup Recipe With Sweet Potato 100
- Skillet Eggs With Salsa Verde 102
- One-Bowl Waffles 104

- Low Fodmap Pesto Pasta With Chicken: 106
- Low Fodmap Baked Cod: 108
- Chicken & Sausage Jambalaya 109
- Quinoa Porridge With Berries And Cinnamon 113
- Carrot Cake With Pecans (8 Servings) 116
- Cinnamon Rolls 119
- Breakfast Pizza 120
- Easy Breakfast Sausage 122
- Orange-Scented Overnight Oatmeal 124
- Hawaiian Toasted Sandwich 126
- Tomato And Green Bean Salad 128
- Maple–Brown Sugar Oatmeal 130
- Quinoa Berry Breakfast Bake 131
- Scrambled Eggs With Smoked Salmon & Cream Cheese 133
- Quinoa Porridge With Berries And Cinnamon 135

KID FRIENDLY LOW FODMAP COOKBOOK

Ingredients:

- Egg
- Olive oil
- Salt and pepper
- Chicken tenders
- Gluten-free breadcrumbs
- Parmesan cheese (optional)

Instructions:

1. Preheat the oven to 425°F (220°C) and line a baking sheet with parchment paper.
2. In a shallow dish, mix breadcrumbs, Parmesan cheese (if using), salt, and pepper.
3. c. In another dish, beat the egg.

4. Dip each chicken tender into the egg, then coat with breadcrumb mixture.
5. e. Place the coated chicken tenders on the baking sheet, drizzle with olive oil, and bake for 15-20 minutes or until golden and cooked through.

Low FODMAP Spaghetti Bolognese:

Ingredients:

- Garlic-infused olive oil
- Fresh basil (chopped)
- Salt and pepper
- Gluten-free spaghetti
- Ground beef
- Tomato passata
- Carrots (peeled and diced)
- Zucchini (diced)

Instructions:

1. a. Cook the gluten-free spaghetti according to package instructions.
2. b. In a large skillet, heat garlic-infused olive oil and sauté carrots and zucchini until tender.
3. c. Add ground beef and cook until browned.

4. d. Pour in tomato passata, season with salt and pepper, and let it simmer for 15-20 minutes.
5. e. Serve the Bolognese sauce over cooked spaghetti and sprinkle with fresh basil.

Grilled Salmon with Lemon:

Ingredients:

- - Dill (fresh or dried)
- Olive oil
- Salt and pepper

Salmon fillets

- Lemon slices

Instructions:

1. Preheat the grill to medium-high heat.
2. Drizzle olive oil over salmon fillets and season with salt, pepper, and dill.
3. c. Place lemon slices on top of each fillet.
4. Grill the salmon for 4-5 minutes per side or until cooked through.

Low FODMAP Chicken Fried Rice:

Ingredients:

- Scallions (green parts only, sliced)
- Eggs (beaten)
- Garlic-infused olive oil
- Gluten-free soy sauce
- Cooked rice (cooled)
- Cooked chicken (diced)
- Carrots (peeled and diced)
- Green beans (cut into small pieces)

Instructions:

a. In a large skillet, heat garlic-infused olive oil and sauté carrots and green beans until tender.

b. Push the vegetables to one side and pour the beaten eggs onto the other side, scrambling them.
c. c. Add diced chicken and cooked rice to the skillet, stirring everything together.
d. Drizzle gluten-free soy sauce over the mixture, tossing well to combine. Cook for another 2-3 minutes until heated through.

Tortilla Baked Eggs

Ingredients

- cherry tomatoes (cut into quarters)
- 1/8 tsp   paprika (small pinch)
- Season with   salt & pepper
- 1 tbsp Colby or cheddar cheese or vegan cheese (optional) (grated)
- 1 tsp   olive oil (for brushing the pan)
- 1 corn tortilla
- 1/2 cup   baby kale or baby spinach (roughly chopped)
- eggs
- 1 tbsp   green onions/scallions (green leaves only, finely chopped)

Instructions:

1. Preheat the oven to 180ºC/350ºF.

2. Roughly chop the spinach or kale. Finely slice the spring onion or green onion. Quarter the cherry tomatoes. Grate the cheese if you're using it.
3. Grease a small oven-proof frypan or baking dish. Make sure the dish is slightly smaller than the tortilla. You can overlap the tortillas in a large dish or use multiple small baking dishes for multiple servings.
4. Gently press the tortilla into the bottom of the dish, like with a pastry sheet. The edges of the tortilla should curl up slightly to form a lip that will hold the eggs.
5. Evenly spread the spinach or kale over the tortilla.
6. Crack the eggs on top, then sprinkle the spring onion, scallion leaves, and chopped tomato— season with a pinch of paprika, salt, and pepper. Add grated cheese if desired.

7. Put the dish in the oven and bake for 15 to 20 minutes till the egg whites are set and no longer jiggly.
8. Remove the low FODMAP tortilla-baked eggs from the oven and transfer them to a dish. Cut into quarters and enjoy!

Asian Chicken Salad

Ingredients

Peanut Butter Dressing:

- 6 tablespoons (102 g) peanut butter, either natural or no-stir style
- 3 tablespoons firmly packed light brown sugar
- 3 tablespoons of rice vinegar or apple cider vinegar
- 3 tablespoons low-sodium gluten-free soy sauce
- 11/2 tablespoons fish sauce
- 1 1/2 tablespoons of freshly squeezed lime juice
- 1 1/2 tablespoons Low Fodmap garlic-Infused Oil
- ¼ to ½ teaspoon sambal oelek or low FODMAP hot sauce

- Water, if needed

Chicken Salad:

- 2 Persian cucumbers, ends trimmed, cut into large julienne
- 1/2 cup (16 g) of chopped fresh cilantro, divided
- 1/2 cup (80 g) chopped roasted peanuts, divided
- 1/2 cup (32 g) chopped scallions, green parts only, divided
- 1 red bell pepper, cored and finely sliced
- pound (455 g) shredded cooked chicken warm or at room temperature
- 4 cups (356 g) finely shredded green cabbage
- 2 medium carrots, trimmed and grated

Instructions:

Peanut Butter Dressing:

1- Combine peanut butter, brown sugar, vinegar, soy sauce, fish sauce, lime juice, oil, and hot sauce in a blender.
2- Blend the ingredients till smooth and well combined, scraping down the sides of the blender as needed.
3- Taste the dressing and add more hot sauce if desired. If using natural peanut butter and the mixture is too thick, blend in a tablespoon or two of water to achieve a smooth and pourable texture.
4- For optimal flavor, the dressing can be made a day ahead and kept in an airtight container in the fridge.

Whole Roast Chicken & Vegetables

Ingredients

- 8- ounces (225 g) trimmed Brussels sprouts, halved lengthwise
- Freshly ground black pepper
- 4 medium carrots, scrubbed, trimmed, cut into 4-inch-long (10 cm) by ½-inch (12 mm) wide pieces
- Kosher salt
- 3 tablespoons extra-virgin olive oil, divided
- 1.6 kg to 2 kg of whole chicken, giblets removed, patted dry
- 2 medium parsnips, scrubbed, trimmed, cut into 4-inch-long (10 cm) by ½-inch (12 mm) wide pieces

Instructions:

1- Pat the chicken dry with paper towels and generously season it with salt inside and out. Secure the legs with kitchen twine and allow the chicken to rest while the oven preheats.

2- Position a rack in the upper third of the oven, ensuring enough space to accommodate the height of the chicken. Place a 12-inch to 14-inch (30.5 cm to 35.5 cm) cast-iron skillet in the oven and preheat it to 425°F (220°C).

3- In the meantime, toss the carrots, parsnips, and Brussels sprouts with half of the olive oil in a large bowl, ensuring all the vegetables are seasoned with salt and pepper to taste.

4- Coat the chicken with some reserved oil once the oven reaches the desired temperature. Drizzle the left-over oil into the hot skillet. Carefully place the chicken in the center of the skillet and scatter the vegetables around it. Roast in the oven for approximately 50 to

60 minutes. Allow the chicken to cool in the skillet for at least 10 minutes.
5- Move the chicken to a cutting board and carve it. Serve the succulent chicken alongside the roasted vegetables.

Bacon and Brie Frittata

Ingredients:

- 100g brie, sliced
- 1 tsp red wine vinegar
- 1 tsp Dijon mustard
- 1 cucumber, halved, deseeded and sliced on the diagonal
- 200g radish, quartered Instructions:
- 2 T olive oil
- 200g smoked bacon
- 6 egg
- lightly beaten
- small bunch chives, snipped

1- teaspoon of oil in a small skillet that is not-stick. Add the bacon and fry until crispy. Place on a paper towel to drain while you do the next step.

2- teaspoons of oil into the same frying pan. Crumble the bacon, add the eggs, chives and black pepper and cook until the eggs are partially set. Now lay the Brie cheese on top. Grill until the eggs are set. Remove the omelet from the pan and cut into 8 wedges, placing 2 on each plate.

3- Mix a salad of the olive oil, vinegar, mustard, seasonings, cucumbers and radishes together and stir to thoroughly saturate the mixture. Place on the plate between the two omelet wedges.

Baked Eggs and Ham Cups (4 servings)

Ingredients:

- 150g of baby spinach
- 4 slices of buttered toast
- 8 Slices of ham
- 2 T grated parmesan cheese
- 4 whole eggs

Instructions:

1. Begin by preheating your oven to 350F degrees. Grease four different oven-safe dishes that can hold ¾ cup, like ramekins. Place 2 slices of ham in each dish, covering the bottom and sides.
2. Microwave your spinach for a minute and a half, then drain it in a colander, pushing and pressing the spinach to remove all excess water.

3. Divide the spinach as evenly as possible between the ramekins, atop the ham slices. Place 2 T of parmesan cheese on the spinach.
4. Break the eggs, one at a time, over each dish gently, so as not to break the yolk. Salt and pepper to taste.
5. Place all the ramekins on one baking tray and place in the oven for fifteen minutes. Bake until the yolks are set to your desired doneness.

Hash Browns

Ingredients:

- 1/4 tsp garlic powder
- 1/4 tsp onion powder
- 1/4 cup vegetable oil
- 2 large russet potatoes, peeled and grated
- 1/4 cup all-purpose flour
- 1/2 tsp salt
- 1/4 tsp black pepper

Instructions:

1- In a large bowl, mix together grated potatoes, flour, salt, black pepper, garlic powder, and onion powder.
2- Drizzle vegetable oil over the mixture and mix well.
3- Form the mixture into small patties and place them into the air fryer basket.

4- Cook at 400°F for 10-15 minutes, or until golden brown and crispy.

Breakfast Sausage

Ingredients:

- 8 breakfast sausages
- 1 tbsp olive oil

Instructions:

1- Brush the sausages with olive oil.
2- Place the sausages into the air fryer basket.
3- Cook at 375°F for 8-10 minutes, or until fully cooked.

Breakfast & Brunch

Cheese, Ham, And Spinach Muffins

Ingredients:

- 6 oz ham, lean
- ¼ cup chopped chives
- ½ cup cheddar cheese, grated (set 2 tbsp aside)
- ¼ cup baby spinach, chopped roughly
- ½ tsp paprika, smoked
- A drizzle of olive oil, used to grease the muffin tins
- ¼ cup oats
- 2 ¼ tsp baking powder
- ½ tsp xanthan gum
- ½ cup thick Greek yogurt
- ⅔ cup lactose-free milk
- 2 large eggs

Instructions:

1- Preheat the oven to 325°F and place a baking tray half-filled with water on the bottom shelf.
2- In a bowl, sift together the flour, baking powder, and xanthan gum, then stir in the oats.
3- In a smaller bowl, whisk the eggs, yogurt, and milk together, then add in the ham, chives, spinach, and cheese.
4- Make a well in the dry mix and pour the wet ingredients into it. Gently fold the ingredients together. The dough should be slightly wet but not liquid.
5- Grease the muffin tin and fill with the mixture. Wet your fingers and tap the top of the tin gently to settle the mixture.
6- Top with the remainder of the cheese and paprika.
7- Bake for 20-25 minutes.

Crunchy Granola

Ingredients:

- 3 tablespoons unrefined coconut oil, liquefied
- 2 teaspoons pure vanilla extract
- 2 teaspoons ground cinnamon
- 1/2 teaspoon sea salt
- 4 cups gluten-free rolled oats
- 1/2 cup sliced almonds
- 1 cup hulled sunflower seeds
- 1/2 cup pure maple syrup

Instructions:

1- Preheat oven to 325°F.
2- Mix all ingredients in a large bowl. Transfer mixture to a baking sheet lined with parchment paper.

3- Cook for 50 minutes, stirring every 10–15 minutes.

Crepes And Berries

Ingredients:

- 1 tsp vanilla extract
- Filling
- ½ cup berry mix
- Pinch of brown sugar
- Pinch of cinnamon
- 2 tbsp Greek yogurt
- Crepes
- ½ cup oat flour
- 1 tsp brown sugar
- 1 tsp white sugar
- 2 eggs
- 1 ½ tbsp melted butter

Instructions:

1. In a blender, place the crepe ingredients and blend for two minutes. Set aside to rest for 15 minutes.
2. Mix the brown sugar and cinnamon with the berries.
3. After the crepe mix has rested, place a non-stick pan, greased with oil, over medium heat. Add ¼ cup of the crepe batter to the pan. Gently move the pan to cover the bottom of the pan with a thin layer of batter. Cook for a minute and gently flip.
4. Once the crepes are cooked, place them on a plate and top with a small amount of yogurt, fold, and place the berries on top.

CHAPTER THREE

CHOCOLATE PANCAKES

Ingredients

- 1 1/3 cups lactose-free milk, whole or 2%, at room temperature
- 4 tablespoons unsalted butter, melted
- 2 large eggs, at room temperature
- 1 teaspoon vanilla extract
- ½ teaspoon instant espresso powder, optional
- 1 ¼ cups gluten-free all-purpose flour
- 1/3 cup Dutch-processed cocoa or Black Cocoa
- 1/3 cup sugar
- 1½ teaspoons baking powder; use gluten-free if following a gluten-free diet
- ½ teaspoon salt

Instructions:

1. Place flour, cocoa, sugar, baking powder, and salt in a large mixing bowl and whisk to aerate and combine. Make a well in the center.
2. Whisk together milk, butter, eggs, vanilla, and espresso powder, if using, in a separate bowl.
3. Pour wet mix over the dry and whisk together until smooth and well combined.
4. Heat electric griddle, heavy sauté pan or nonstick pan. Coat with nonstick spray and heat until a few drops of water dance. Dole out about 3 tablespoon amounts of batter at a time (we use an ice cream scoop) and cook over medium heat until bubbles begin to appear here and there, about 1 minute or so.
5. Usually I tell you to check the bottoms for a golden brown color, but these pancakes are super dark, so you have to use other cues. You can gently lift one and check; the bottom should be dry. Flip over and cook for about 1

minute more or until that side is cooked through as well.

6. Serve hot with real maple syrup or lactose-free ice cream and Salted Caramel Sauce, if you dare.

CORNBREAD MUFFINS

Ingredients

- 1 tablespoon plus 1 teaspoon baking powder, use gluten-free if following a gluten-free diet
- 1 teaspoon salt
- 4 tablespoons unsalted butter, melted
- 1/4 cup neutral flavored oil, such as canola or vegetable
- 2 large eggs, at room temperature
- 1½ cups lactose-free whole milk, at room temperature
- 1 tablespoon plus 1 teaspoon lemon juice
- 1¾ cups fine stoneground yellow cornmeal
- 1 cup gluten-free all-purpose flour
- 1/3 cup sugar

Instructions:

1. Position rack in center of oven. Preheat oven to 400°F/200°C. Coat 12 muffin wells with nonstick spray; set aside.
2. Stir the milk and lemon juice together in a medium-sized bowl and allow to sit for 5 minutes to thicken while oven preheats.
3. Whisk together the cornmeal, flour, sugar, baking powder and salt in a large mixing bowl to aerate and combine. Make a small well in the center and set aside.
4. Whisk the melted butter, vegetable oil and eggs into the thickened milk until combined. Pour this wet mixture into the well of the dry mix and whisk together just until combined. Divide evenly into prepared pan.
5. Bake for about 14 to 18 minutes or just until a toothpick inserted in the center comes out clean. Cool pan(s) on rack for 2 minutes, then unmold onto rack. Muffins are ready to eat while warm or cool to room temperature and

store in airtight containers at room temperature for up to 2 days; they do dry out a bit. Muffins may also be frozen in heavy zip top bags for up to 1 month

GREEN KIWI SMOOTHIE

Ingredients

- inches (20 cm) of unpeeled English, hothouse style cucumber, cut into chunks
- 2 cups (40 g) baby spinach, (for a milder taste) or chopped stemmed, washed and dried Lacinato kale leaves (for a bolder taste) or a combo
- 1 ½ to 2 cups ice cubes
- 1 cup (170 g) seedless green grapes
- 1 kiwi, peeled and cut into chunks
- 2 tablespoons water

Instructions:

1. Place all the items in blender in order listed except the ice. Pulse on an off to begin blending, then blend on high speed until

puréed, blended and smooth. Add the smaller amount of ice cubes and blend until frosty, pulsing on and off.

2. Add more ice cubes if desired. Serve immediately as it separates upon sitting. It will still be good, just not as pretty.

LOW FODMAP RECIPES

Greek-style roasted chicken with lemon and oregano

Ingredients:

- 1 tablespoon dried oregano
- 1 teaspoon dried thyme
- 1 teaspoon paprika
- Salt and pepper to taste
- Fresh oregano leaves for garnish (optional)
- 1 whole chicken (about 4-5 lbs)
- 1/4 cup olive oil
- Juice of 1 lemon
- Zest of 1 lemon
- 4 cloves garlic, minced

Instructions:

1. Preheat the oven to 425°F (220°C).

2. Rinse the chicken and pat it dry with paper towels.
3. In a small bowl, whisk together the olive oil, lemon juice, lemon zest, minced garlic, dried oregano, dried thyme, paprika, salt, and pepper to create a marinade.
4. Place the chicken in a roasting pan or baking dish.
5. Pour the marinade over the chicken, making sure to coat it evenly, including the cavity.
6. Place the chicken in the preheated oven and roast for about 1 hour to 1 hour 15 minutes, or until the internal temperature reaches 165°F (74°C) when measured with a meat thermometer inserted into the thickest part of the thigh without touching the bone.
7. While roasting, baste the chicken with the pan juices every 20-30 minutes to keep it moist and flavorful.

8. Once cooked, remove the chicken from the oven and let it rest for 10-15 minutes before carving.
9. Garnish with fresh oregano leaves, if desired.
10. Serve the Greek-style roasted chicken with lemon and oregano hot.
11. Enjoy this succulent and aromatic chicken with a taste of the Mediterranean!

Grilled Chicken with Roasted Vegetables:

Ingredients:

- 4 chicken breasts
- 2 zucchini, sliced
- 2 red bell peppers, sliced
- 1 eggplant, sliced
- Olive oil
- Salt and pepper to taste

Instructions:

1. Preheat the grill to medium-high heat.
2. Brush the chicken breasts with olive oil and season with salt and pepper.
3. Grill the chicken for 6-8 minutes per side, or until cooked through.
4. Meanwhile, preheat the oven to 400°F (200°C).

5. Place the sliced zucchini, red bell peppers, and eggplant on a baking sheet.
6. Drizzle with olive oil and season with salt and pepper.
7. Roast in the oven for 20-25 minutes, or until the vegetables are tender.
8. Serve the grilled chicken with the roasted vegetables.

Low FODMAP Buffalo Chicken Dip

Ingredients

- 1 cup Green valley lactose unfastened cream cheese
- 2 cups shredded Cheddar cheese
- ¼ chopped cup green onion/scallions (green element only)
- 12 oz. Boneless hen breasts, cooked and shredded
- ¼ cup warm sauce (without garlic, onion such as Texas Petes)
- 1 cup Green Valley lactose unfastened sour cream

Instructions

1. Preheat oven to 350 degrees F.

2. Combine shredded hen, warm sauce, bitter cream, cream cheese, 1 1/2 cups of the Cheddar cheese and a pair of tablespoons of the green onion.

3. Spread dip right into a small casserole dish and top with remaining cheddar cheese.

4. Bake for 25 mins or until dip is excellent and bubbly.

5. Garnish with last inexperienced onion.

6. Serve with child carrots, bell peppers strips, and corn tortilla chips!

Low FODMAP Antipasto Skewers

Ingredients

- Thinly sliced prosciutto, reduce in thirds lengthwise
- Fresh basil leaves, washed and sliced in half
- 1 small field grape tomatoes
- small bamboo skewers approximately 6 inches lengthy
- 1 small jar peperoncini
- 1 small jar pitted Kalamata olives
- 1 small container clean small mozzarella balls

Instructions

1. If pepperoncini are large, reduce in half
2. Fold prosciutto into layered square to healthy on skewer.
3. Thread ingredients on skewer as preferred.
4. Serve on platter!

Lemon Parsley Roasted Shrimp

Ingredients

- 2 tablespoons lemon juice
- 1/2 teaspoon overwhelmed pink pepper flakes
- sea salt and pepper, to taste
- 1/4 cup shredded Parmesan
- 1/4 freshly chopped parsley
- 1 pound greater big shrimp (peeled and deveined, can leave tail shell on, if desired)
- 2 tablespoons garlic infused oil

Instructions

1. Preheat oven to 400 tiers F.
2. Lightly oil cookie sheet.
3. Pat shrimp dry with paper towel and add to cookie sheet in even layer.

4. In small bowl, whisk together oil, lemon, beaten red pepper, sea salt and pepper, to taste and drizzle evenly over shrimp.
5. Roast shrimp for 6-eight mins, until cooked thru and opaque.
6. Remove shrimp from oven and sprinkle with shredded Parmesan and sparkling parsley.

Parmesan Roasted Broccoli

Ingredients

- 1/3 cup Parmesan cheese
- 1/3 cup almond flour (I used Bob's Red Mill first-rate-first-class almond flour)
- 3 cups broccoli florets
- 2 eggs

Instructions

1. Preheat oven to 350 tiers F and lightly oil baking sheet.
2. In small bowl, whisk both eggs to combination.
3. On large plate or in a plastic bag, mix Parmesan and almond flour.
4. Dip approximately 1 broccoli florets in egg, then upload to Parmesan and almond flour aggregate to lightly coat.

5. Place broccoli on baking sheet. Repeat technique with last broccoli.
6. Place in oven and bake for 15-20 mins. Turn broccoli during mid-point of cooking time.

Orange Cranberry Walnut Scones

Ingredients

- 2 teaspoons orange zest
- 1/4 cup dried cranberries, finely chopped
- 1/4 cup walnuts, finely chopped
- Orange glaze:
- 2/3 cup confectioner's sugar
- 1 teaspoon orange zest
- 1 1/2 tablespoons freshly squeezed orange juice
- 2 mini scones or one medium sized scone.
- 16 mini scones; 12 medium scones.
- 2 cups gluten loose flour mixture (along with King Arthur GF measure for measure or Bob's Red Mill GF 1 for 1)

- 1 1/2 teaspoon baking powder (use gluten unfastened if following gluten loose food regimen)
- half of teaspoon baking soda
- half cup sugar
- 1 massive egg
- 1/4 cup sour cream (this can provide minimal lactose per serving)
- 12 tablespoons bloodless unsalted butter

Instructions

1. Preheat oven to four hundred stages F.
2. Prepare scone pan if the use of or add parchment paper to baking sheet.
3. In big bowl, add flour combo, baking powder, soda and sugar. Set aside.
4. In small bowl, mix egg and sour cream, set aside.

5. Slice butter in chew length pieces and add to flour aggregate. Using pastry blender or palms, mix butter into flour mixture until the mixture resembles direction crumbs.
6. Add sour cream and egg combination to flour mixture.
7. Fold in orange zest, cranberries and walnuts.
8. If the use of mini scone pan, add dough frivolously to pan. If making scones into rounds, divide dough in half. Make 2 small rounds along with your arms. Cut every spherical into 6 triangular fashioned scones (like slicing a pie) and place scones on baking sheet approximately an inch apart.
9. Bake scones for 15 minutes. The scones need to be gently browned on the edges.
10. While scones cool, make orange glaze. Simply add confectioner's sugar, zest and orange juice and blend with a fork until combined. Drizzle over scones.

Dry belly soup with cabbage and celery

Ingredients:

- 2 green peppers
- Salt to taste
- Pepper to taste
- Oregano to taste
- 1/2 chopped cabbage
- 6 large chopped onions
- 6 tomatoes chopped without seeds
- 3 stalks of celery

Instructions:

1. Wash vegetables and chop as instructed above. Bring all of these ingredients into a pan with water to cover.

2. Let it cook over medium-high heat with the pan semi-capped.

3. Season with salt, pepper and oregano and other spices and herbs you prefer.

4. Cook until the vegetables are tender. Serve immediately.

Dry Soup Recipe for Pumpkin Belly

Ingredients:

- 1/2 Japanese Pumpkin
- 0.19 inch ginger, without chopped peel
- 1 chopped onion
- 3 cloves garlic, crushed
- 3 stalks of holy grass
- 1 1/2 l of water
- Olive oil to taste

Instructions:

1. Wash the pumpkin in running water. In a pan, put 2 cups water, the pumpkin and lightly cook over medium heat for 10 minutes.
2. Meanwhile, wash, peel and slice the ginger. Peel garlic and onion cut the onion into 4 parts.

3. Transfer pre-cooked squash to a board and, with the vegetable peeler, remove the peel. Reserve the cooking water. Cut the pumpkin into cubes and return to the pan with the water. Add the ginger, the garlic, the onion, the holy grass and the rest of the water. Bring to the medium heat and cook with the pan covered for 40 minutes.
4. After this time, remove the stalks of holy grass. Transfer to the blender and beat everything. Season with little salt and pepper to taste return the soup to the pan to heat and serve them.

CORNBREAD WAFFLES

Ingredients:

- 1 teaspoon of salt
- 4 tablespoons (57 g) of unsalted butter
- 2 cups (480 ml) of lactose-free whole milk, 2%, 1% or reduced fat, at room temperature
- 2 large eggs, at room temperature
- 1 teaspoon of vanilla extract
- 1 ⅔ cups (241 g) of LOW FODMAP, gluten-free all-purpose flour, such as Bob's Red Mill Gluten-Free 1 to 1 Baking Flour
- 1¼ cups (173 g) of fine ground yellow cornmeal, preferably stone ground
- 1 tablespoon of baking powder (use gluten-free if following a gluten-free diet)
- 1 tablespoon of sugar

Instructions:

1. Preheat the waffle iron according to the instructions provided by the manufacturer.
2. If you wish to keep the waffles warm between batches, preheat the oven to 200°F/95°C.
3. In a large mixing bowl, whisk together the flour, cornmeal, baking powder, sugar, and salt to combine and aerate the mixture. Create a well in the center and set it aside.
4. In a microwave-safe bowl, melt the butter in the microwave. Then, stir in the milk and eggs until thoroughly blended. Alternatively, you can melt the butter in a small skillet over low-medium heat on the stovetop, transfer it to a mixing bowl, and proceed with adding the milk and eggs.
5. Pour the wet mixture into the well in the dry mixture and whisk gently until just

incorporated, ensuring there are no pockets of flour. The batter will be thick.
6. Lightly coat the waffle maker with nonstick spray (you may only need to do this once). Scoop the waffle batter onto the hot waffle iron, making sure it covers the entire surface without overfilling. Close the top and cook until the waffles are crispy on both sides and golden brown. This usually takes around 4 minutes, depending on the waffle maker. As you continue making waffles, keep them warm in the oven directly on a rack. Serve the waffles immediately with pure maple syrup and a dollop of butter. You can also add fruit if you like.

LOW FODMAP BREAKFAST PORK SAUSAGE PATTIES

Ingredients:

- 1 teaspoon crushed fennel seeds
- ½ teaspoon chili powder, such as powdered red serrano chili
- ¼ teaspoon paprika
- Freshly ground black pepper
- 1 pound (455 g) ground pork
- 1 tablespoon firmly packed light brown sugar
- 1 tablespoon coarsely chopped fresh sage or 1 teaspoon rubbed (ground) sage
- 1 tablespoon coarsely chopped fresh thyme or 1 teaspoon dried thyme
- 1 ¼ teaspoons kosher salt

Instructions:

1. In a medium-sized mixing bowl, combine brown sugar, sage, thyme, salt, fennel seeds, chili powder, paprika, and black pepper. Use your fingers to massage the mixture together to ensure all the herbs and spices are well blended.
2. Add the ground pork to the mixture and mix everything together until well combined. (You can prepare this mixture the night before by covering the dish with plastic wrap.)
3. Use a ¼ cup (60 ml) measuring cup or an ice cream scoop of comparable size to shape the patties. Flatten them to approximately ¼-inch (6 mm) thickness. Note that they will expand in thickness during cooking.
4. Heat a cast iron or heavy skillet over medium-high heat. Cook the patties for about 2 to 3 minutes on each side until golden brown. Ensure that the patties are cooked thoroughly.

5. The sausages are now ready to serve. They can also be frozen by cooling them first, arranging them in single layers separated by parchment paper in an airtight container, and freezing for up to 1 month. You can cook them on the stovetop in a skillet or in the microwave.

Cheesy Frittata

Ingredients:

- 1 cup of potatoes (cooked, sliced)
- 2 eggs (beaten)
- 2 spring onions (sliced finely)
- pepper
- salt
- 1 tbsp dill (fresh, roughly chopped)
- 1 tbsp olive oil
- ¼ cup of cheddar cheese (grated)

Instructions:

1. In a pan, add the oil over medium heat.
2. When the oil is hot enough, add the potatoes. Fry for about 8 minutes until the potatoes start crisping up.

3. In a bowl, add the eggs, dill, spring onions, salt, and pepper. Whisk well.
4. Pour the egg mixture into the pan and mix everything together.
5. Sprinkle cheese all over the eggs and potatoes. Cook for about 8 minutes.
6. Flip the frittata over and continue cooking for about 4 minutes.
7. Transfer the frittata to a plate.
8. Slice and serve immediately.

Sweet and Savory Corn Bread

Ingredients :

- ¼ tsp baking soda
- ⅛ cup of vegetable oil
- ⅓ cup of low-FODMAP all-purpose flour (gluten-free)
- ¾ cup of buttermilk (lactose-free)
- ¾ cup of medium-grind cornmeal
- 1 large egg
- 3 slices of meaty bacon
-
- 1 ¼ tsp baking powder
- ⅛ cup of pure maple syrup
- ⅛ cup of scallions (green parts, chopped)

Ingredients For The Glaze:

- ½ tbsp butter (unsalted, melted)

- ½ tbsp pure maple syrup

Instructions:

1. Preheat your oven to 425 °F. Place a rack in the middle of the oven.
2. In a skillet, add the bacon over low-medium heat.
3. Cook both sides of the bacon until crispy.
4. After cooking, transfer the bacon to a plate lined with a paper towel.
5. Drain the bacon grease from the skillet but leave around 1 tbsp for the next step.
6. In a bowl, add the baking powder, baking soda, cornmeal, and salt. Mix well.
7. In another bowl, add the maple syrup, buttermilk, eggs, and oil. Whisk well.
8. Pour the mixture into the bowl with the dry ingredients and mix until well combined.
9. Fold the scallions into the mixture.

10. Add the bacon back into the skillet, then pour the mixture over it. Use a spatula to spread the mixture evenly around the skillet.
11. Place the skillet in the oven. Bake the corn bread for about 25–30 minutes.
12. After baking, take the skillet out of the oven.
13. Allow the corn bread to cool down for about 5 minutes.
14. In the meantime, combine the glaze ingredients and mix well.
15. Transfer the corn bread to a plate and drizzle the glaze over it.
16. Serve while warm.

Low FODMAP Mini Pizzas:

Ingredients:

- Mozzarella cheese
- Sliced pepperoni
- Gluten-free pizza crusts
- Low FODMAP pizza sauce

Instructions:

1. a. Preheat the oven according to the pizza crust instructions.
2. Spread the low FODMAP pizza sauce over each pizza crust.
3. c. Sprinkle mozzarella cheese on top and add sliced pepperoni.
4. Bake the mini pizzas according to the pizza crust instructions or until the cheese is melted and bubbly.

Low FODMAP Turkey Tacos:

Ingredients:

- Shredded cheddar cheese
- Fresh cilantro (chopped)
- Lime wedges
- Salt and pepper
- Ground turkey
- Corn tortillas
- Lettuce (shredded)
- Tomatoes (diced)

Instructions:

1. In a skillet, cook the ground turkey until browned, breaking it up into crumbles.
2. Warm the corn tortillas in a dry skillet or microwave.

3. Assemble the tacos by placing cooked turkey on each tortilla.
4. Top with shredded lettuce, diced tomatoes, shredded cheddar cheese, and fresh cilantro.
5. Squeeze lime juice over the tacos and season with salt and pepper to taste.

Low FODMAP Veggie Stir-Fry:

Ingredients:

- Gluten-free soy sauce
- Garlic-infused olive oil
- Sesame seeds (optional)
- Cooked rice or rice noodles Firm tofu (cut into cubes)
- Carrots (peeled and thinly sliced)
- Bell peppers (sliced)
- Green beans
- Bok choy (sliced)

Instructions:

1. In a large skillet or wok, heat garlic-infused olive oil and sauté carrots, bell peppers, and green beans until tender.
2. Add bok choy and tofu cubes, stirring gently to combine.

3. Drizzle gluten-free soy sauce over the mixture and cook until heated through.

4. Serve over cooked rice or rice noodles and sprinkle with sesame seeds if desired.

Low FODMAP Chicken and Rice Soup:

Ingredients:

- Low FODMAP chicken broth
- Cooked rice
- Fresh parsley (chopped)
- Salt and pepper
- Cooked chicken (shredded)
- Carrots (peeled and diced)
- Green beans (cut into small pieces)

Instructions:

1. In a soup pot, combine shredded chicken, carrots, and green beans.
2. Pour in low FODMAP chicken broth and bring to a boil. Reduce heat and let it simmer until the vegetables are tender.

3. Add cooked rice and stir to combine.
4. Season with salt and pepper to taste and garnish with chopped parsley.

Berry Nice Muesli

Ingredients

- 4 tbsp   olive oil
- 2 tbsp   brown sugar
- 1 1/2 tsp   vanilla extract
- 8 tbsp   dried cranberries
- 12 g (1 cup) freeze-dried strawberries (chopped)
- 300 g (3 cups) rolled oats
- 80 g (1 cup) dried shredded coconut
- 115 g (1 cup) pecan (chopped)
- 105 g (3/4 cup) pumpkin seeds
- 4 tbsp   pure maple syrup

Instructions:

1. Heat the oven to 160ºC/320ºF and line a deep roasting tray with baking paper.

2. Mix the maple syrup, olive oil, brown sugar, and vanilla in a small bowl.
3. Combine the oats, coconut, chopped pecans, and pumpkin seeds in a bowl. Pour in the sugar mixture and mix everything.
4. Pour the oat mixture into the prepared roasting tray, spreading it evenly in a shallow layer. Put the tray in the middle of the oven and bake for 20 minutes. Then, stir it and continue baking for another 10 to 15 minutes till it turns golden.
5. Remove the tray from the oven and carefully mix in the dried cranberries and strawberries.
6. Allow the mixture to cool, then move it to an airtight container. It can be stored for up to three weeks.
7. When ready to enjoy, serve ¾ cup portions with your choice of low-FODMAP milk and yogurt.

Macaroni Slaw

Ingredients

- 2 medium carrots, scrubbed, root end trimmed, shredded
- 2 medium stalks of celery, diced
- 1/4 cup (16 g) finely chopped scallions, green parts only
- 1 teaspoon celery seeds
- 1/4 cup (60 ml) of apple cider vinegar
- Kosher salt
- Freshly ground black pepper
- 12 ounces (340 g) low FODMAP gluten-free elbow pasta, cooked al dente, drained, and cooled
- 1/4 cup (60 g) lactose-free sour cream

- 1 cup (226 g) of mayonnaise
- 8 ounces (225 g) green cabbage, shredded
- 1 tablespoon sugar
- 1 medium green bell pepper, cored and diced
- 8 ounces (225 g) of red cabbage, shredded

Instructions:

1. Combine the drained and cooled pasta, red and green cabbage, shredded carrot, diced celery, bell pepper, and chopped scallions in a mixing bowl.
2. Whisk together the mayo, vinegar, sour cream, sugar, and celery seed in a small mixing bowl. Taste the dressing and adjust the seasoning with salt and pepper according to your preference.
3. Pour the dressing directly over the pasta and vegetables, and gently fold everything until well mixed.

4. The salad is ready to be served, but let it sit for at least 1 hour for the best flavor to allow the flavors to meld together. Alternatively, you can refrigerate the salad overnight in an airtight container.
5. Before serving, let the salad cool to room temperature or serve it lightly chilled for optimal enjoyment.
6. The salad can be stored in the fridge for up to three days in an airtight container.

reakfast Burrito

Ingredients:

- 1/4 cup diced tomatoes
- 1/4 cup diced onions
- 1/4 cup diced green bell peppers
- Salt and pepper to taste
- 2 large flour tortillas
- 4 large eggs
- 1/4 cup milk
- 1/2 cup shredded cheddar cheese
- 2 slices of bacon, cooked and crumbled

Instructions:

1. In a bowl, whisk together eggs, milk, salt, and pepper.
2. Add in shredded cheese, crumbled bacon, diced tomatoes, onions, and green bell peppers.

3. Spoon the mixture onto the center of each tortilla and fold into a burrito.
4. Place the burritos into the air fryer basket and cook at 350°F for 8-10 minutes, or until golden brown.

Potatoes

Ingredients:

- 1/2 tsp onion powder
- 1/2 tsp paprika
- Salt and pepper to taste
- 4 medium potatoes, peeled and diced
- 1 tbsp olive oil
- 1/2 tsp garlic powder

Instructions:

1. In a large bowl, mix together diced potatoes, olive oil, garlic powder, onion powder, paprika, salt, and pepper.
2. Place the potatoes into the air fryer basket.
3. Cook at 400°F for 18-20 minutes, or until golden brown and crispy.

Breakfast Quesadilla

Ingredients:

- 1/4 cup diced tomatoes
- 1/4 cup diced onions
- 1/4 cup diced green bell peppers
- 2 large flour tortillas
- 4 large eggs, scrambled
- 1/2 cup shredded cheddar cheese
- 2 slices of bacon, cooked and crumbled

Instructions:

1. Place one tortilla in the air fryer basket.
2. Add scrambled eggs, shredded cheese, crumbled bacon, diced tomatoes, onions, and green bell peppers on top of the tortilla.
3. Place the second tortilla on top of the filling.
4. Cook at 350°F for 5-7 minutes, or until the tortilla is golden brown and crispy.

Cheesy Corn Muffins

Ingredients:

- 3 large eggs
- ½ cup (2 ounces/60 g) grated cheddar, plus twelve ⅓-inch (1 cm) cubes
- ½ cup (1½ ounces/40 g) finely grated Parmesan
- 4 to 6 lean bacon slices (4 ounces/115 g), cooked until crispy (see Instructions: under Bacon and Zucchini Crustless Quiche) and crumbled (optional)
- 1 cup (200 g) drained canned or thawed frozen corn kernels
- Pinch of salt and freshly ground black pepper
- ½ cup (75 g) cornstarch
- ½ cup (65 g) tapioca flour
- 2 teaspoons gluten-free baking powder

- 1 teaspoon baking soda
- 1 teaspoon xanthan gum or guar gum
- 3 tablespoons (45 g) salted butter, melted
- ¾ cup (200 g) gluten-free low-fat plain yogurt

Instructions:

1. Preheat the oven to 325°F (170°C) and line a 12-cup muffin pan with paper liners.
2. Sift the rice flour, cornstarch, tapioca flour, baking powder, baking soda, and xanthan gum three times into a large bowl (or whisk in the bowl until well combined).
3. Combine the melted butter, yogurt, eggs, cheddar, Parmesan, bacon (if using), and corn in a medium bowl. Add the yogurt mixture to the flour mixture and stir with a large metal spoon until just combined (do not overmix). Season with salt and pepper. Half-fill the muffin cups with the batter, then place a cube

of cheddar in each one. Pour in the remaining batter until the cups are two-thirds full.

4. Bake for 15 to 20 minutes, until firm to the touch and a toothpick inserted into the center of a muffin (avoid the cheese filling) comes out clean. Cool in the pan for 5 minutes, then turn out onto a wire rack to cool completely.

Crispy Rice Balls With Parmesan And Corn

Ingredients:

- ¾ cup (150 g) canned corn kernels, drained
- 1 large egg, beaten
- 1⅓ cups (160 g) dried gluten-free, soy-free bread crumbs*
- Canola oil, for pan-frying
- 3 cups (750 ml) gluten-free, onion-free chicken or vegetable stock*
- ¾ cup (150 g) long-grain white or brown rice
- ¾ cup (2 ounces/60 g) grated Parmesan

Instructions:

1. Pour the stock into a large saucepan and bring to a boil. Add the rice and cook until tender, 10 to 12 minutes for white rice, 45 to 50 minutes for brown. Drain and return to the

pan. While the rice is still warm, stir in the Parmesan and corn. Transfer to a bowl and set aside to cool to room temperature.

2. Preheat the oven to 300°F (150°C).
3. Roll the cooled rice mixture into about 30 golf ball–size balls. Dip the balls in the beaten egg, then roll in the bread crumbs until well coated.
4. Heat a little canola oil in a medium frying pan over medium-high heat. Working in batches of 10, add the rice balls to the pan and cook, turning regularly, until nicely browned all over. Set aside on a baking sheet and keep warm in the oven while you make the rest, adding more oil if needed. Serve warm.

Vegetable curry with quinoa

Ingredients:

- 1 cup cauliflower florets
- 1 can (14 oz) coconut milk
- 2 tablespoons curry powder
- 1 teaspoon ground cumin
- 1/2 teaspoon ground turmeric
- Salt and pepper to taste
- Fresh cilantro for garnish
- 1 cup cooked quinoa
- 2 tablespoons olive oil
- 1 onion, diced
- 2 cloves garlic, minced
- 1 tablespoon grated ginger
- 1 bell pepper, diced
- 1 zucchini, diced
- 1 carrot, diced

Instructions:

1. Heat the olive oil in a large pot or skillet over medium heat.
2. Add the diced onion, minced garlic, and grated ginger to the pot. Cook for 2-3 minutes, until fragrant.
3. Add the diced bell pepper, diced zucchini, diced carrot, and cauliflower florets to the pot. Stir and cook for 5-7 minutes, until the vegetables start to soften.
4. In a small bowl, whisk together the curry powder, ground cumin, ground turmeric, salt, and pepper.
5. Add the spice mixture to the pot and stir well to coat the vegetables.
6. Pour in the coconut milk and bring the mixture to a simmer.
7. Reduce the heat to low and let the curry simmer for 15-20 minutes, allowing the

flavors to meld together and the vegetables to become tender.
8. Stir in the cooked quinoa and cook for an additional 2-3 minutes to heat through.
9. Season with salt and pepper to taste.
10. Serve the vegetable curry with quinoa hot.
11. Garnish with fresh cilantro for added freshness and flavor.
12. Enjoy this flavorful and hearty vegetable curry with quinoa!

Chocolate Avocado Waffles

Ingredients

- 1 cup Gluten Free Waffle Mix (I used my DIY Low FODMAP & Gluten Free Waffle Mix-seek my blog)
- 2/3 cup lactose free milk
- 2 tablespoons semi-candy chocolate morsels
- Dress up with butter, strawberry slices and sprinkle of confectioner's sugar
- 1 cup Gluten Free Waffle Mix (I used my DIY Low FODMAP & Gluten Free Waffle Mix-seek my blog)
- 2/3 cup lactose free milk
- 2 tablespoons semi-candy chocolate morsels
- Dress up with butter, strawberry slices and sprinkle of confectioner's sugar

- Makes 4 waffles--serving length 1 waffle
- 2 tablespoons ripe avocado, mashed
- 1/4 cup cocoa (I used Hershey's Cocoa--special dark)
- 1 big egg

Instructions

1. Prepare waffle maker by using lightly oiling and heating as directed.
2. In medium bowl, upload mashed avocado, cocoa powder and egg, mixing to combo.
3. Add in waffle mix and milk, stirring till mixture is clean.
4. Fold in semi-sweet chocolate morsels.
5. Pour batter into waffle maker and cook as directed on waffle maker (times may also range depending on length of waffles)
6. Dress up waffles with butter, strawberry slices and confectioner's sugar, as preferred.

DIY Low FODMAP & Gluten Free Waffle Mix

Ingredients

- 1 half teaspoons baking powder (use gluten loose if following gluten free food plan)
- 1 teaspoon baking soda
- half teaspoon salt
- 3 cups gluten loose flour
- 1/3 cup sugar

Instructions

1. Add the gluten free flour combination, sugar, baking powder, baking soda and salt into a large glass Mason jar or comparable sealed container.

To make 4 waffles:

2. In medium bowl, add 1 cup of waffle blend, 1 egg, 1 half of tablespoons vegetable oil or melted butter, 2/3 cup of lactose unfastened milk

Gluten Free Egg and Cheese Soufflé

Ingredients

- This recipe is gluten free but does comprise trace ability FODMAPs in Worcestershire sauce
- five Slices Udi's GF bread (White sandwich bread is low FODMAP)
- 2 tablespoons butter
- 4 eggs
- 2 cups milk (use lactose free if lactose intolerance)
- 1 cup preferred GF cheese (cheddar, pepper jack works well)
- 1 ½ tsp. Lea and Perrin's Worcestershire Sauce (It's GF too)

- 1 ½ tsp. Yellow mustard (check elements to ensure its GF mustard)
- 1-2 tsp. Sparkling chives, finely chopped

Instructions

1. Butter bread and reduce into cubes (about 6 cubes in step with slice.)
2. Add buttered bread cubes to 8 x 8 casserole dish or 9 inch round casserole
3. Whip eggs, milk, Worcestershire sauce and mustard together.
4. Pour egg combination over bread, cover tightly with plastic wrap and refrigerate overnight.
5. Preheat oven to 350 levels and bake for 55 mins till cooked thru and barely browned on pinnacle.

Dry belly soup recipe with cabbage

Ingredients:

- oz. of the pod
- 2 cabbage leaves chopped into strips
- 1 chopped onion
- 1 tablespoon of olive oil
- Salt to taste
- 1 chopped carrot
- 1 chopped turnip greens
- 2 tomatoes chopped without seeds
- 1/2 chopped cabbage into strips

Instructions:

1. Put the olive oil to heat in a pan. When golden, place the carrot and turnip and cover with 500 ml of water and cook for 20 minutes.

Add the remaining ingredients, add more water if necessary and bring to the boil for 10 minutes. Set seasonings and serve!

Dry belly soup recipe with sweet potato

Ingredients:

- 1 medium sweet potato chopped;
- 2 cups chopped spinach
- Chopped parsley to taste
- 1 liter of water
- Salt to taste
- 1 tablespoon of olive oil;
- 2 cloves garlic, minced;
- 1 medium chopped onion;
- 3 tomatoes skinless and chopped seeds;
- 2 chopped zucchini;

Instructions:

1. Inside a saucepan, heat the olive oil and then sauté the garlic, onion, and tomato.
2. Add zucchini, peeled and chopped sweet potatoes and spinach and cook for 5 minutes.
3. Wait for the soup to simmer and beat in the blender until you get a creamy soup.
4. Return to the pot to heat, season seasoning if necessary and serve with fresh parsley.

Skillet Eggs With Salsa Verde

Ingredients:

- black pepper
- 1 tbsp cilantro (fresh, chopped, for serving)
- ⅛ cup Oaxaca cheese (grated, for serving)
- 4 corn tortillas (warmed, for serving)
- 1 tsp garlic-infused olive oil
- 1 tbsp jalapeño (fresh, minced)
- ¼ cup of salsa verde (homemade or store-bought)
- 2 large eggs

Instructions:

1. In a skillet, add the olive oil over medium heat.

2. When the oil is hot enough, add the jalapeño. Cook for about 2–3 minutes until the pieces of jalapeño soften.
3. Add the salsa verde and mix well.
4. Gently crack the eggs into the skillet.
5. Cover the skillet and allow the eggs to cook for about 5–8 minutes depending on your preference.
6. Take the lid off the skillet. Season the eggs with pepper, then top with cheese and cilantro.
7. Serve immediately with warm tortillas.

One-Bowl Waffles

Ingredients:

- ½ cup of almond milk
- ¾ cup of low-FODMAP waffle mix (like Bisquick gluten-free mix)
- 1 egg
- maple syrup (for serving)
- ½ tsp vanilla extract
- 1 ½ tbsp vegetable oil
- ¼ cup of mini chocolate chips (dairy-free, semisweet)

Instructions:

1. In a bowl, add the egg and almond milk. Whisk well.
2. Add the oil and waffle mix, then continue whisking until well combined.
3. Add the vanilla extract and mix well.

4. Fold the chocolate chips into the mixture.
5. Warm up your waffle maker.
6. When it's warm enough, pour batter into it. Cook the waffles according to the instructions of your waffle maker.
7. Serve immediately with maple syrup and desired toppings.

Low FODMAP Pesto Pasta with Chicken:

Ingredients:

- Cherry tomatoes (halved)
- Olive oil
- Fresh basil leaves (optional)
- Gluten-free pasta (e.g., penne or fusilli)
- Cooked chicken (diced)
- Pesto sauce (check for garlic and onion-free options)

Instructions:

1. Cook the gluten-free pasta according to package instructions.
2. In a large skillet, heat olive oil and sauté diced cooked chicken until warmed.
3. c. Add halved cherry tomatoes and cook for another minute.

4. Toss the cooked pasta with pesto sauce in the skillet until well coated.
5. e. Serve with fresh basil leaves on top if desired.

Low FODMAP Baked Cod:

Ingredients:

- Fresh dill (chopped)
- Olive oil
- Salt and pepper
- Cod fillets
- Lemon juice

Instructions:

1. Preheat the oven to 400°F (200°C) and line a baking dish with parchment paper.
2. Place the cod fillets in the baking dish.
3. Drizzle lemon juice and olive oil over the fillets.
4. Season with fresh dill, salt, and pepper.
5. e. Bake for 15-20 minutes or until the fish is cooked through and flakes easily with a fork.

Chicken & Sausage Jambalaya

Ingredients

- 2 cups (370 g) long-grain white rice
- 6 medium chicken thighs, skin on, bone in
- 2 teaspoons paprika
- 2 teaspoons kosher salt
- 1 teaspoon black pepper
- 1 teaspoon oregano
- 1 teaspoon thyme
- ¼ to 1 teaspoon chipotle chile powder
- 4 cups (960 ml) water
- 1, 28 ounce (793 g) can of diced tomatoes, preferably fire-roasted
- 1 pound (455 g) low FODMAP sausage (we used a sweet sausage)
- 1/4 cup (60 ml) Low Fodmap garlic-Infused Oil

- 1 medium green bell pepper cored, seeded, and diced
- 1/2 cup (36 g) chopped leeks, green parts only
- 1/2 cup (32 g) chopped scallions, green parts only
- 1 medium celery stalk, diced
- 1 bay leaf

Instructions:

1. Mix the chicken thighs with paprika, salt, pepper, oregano, thyme, and chipotle chile in a mixing bowl. Toss the chicken thighs in the spice mixture until they are well coated. Set it aside.
2. Bring water or stock to a boil over medium heat in a medium-sized saucepan. Prick the sausages in a few places and add them to the boiling liquid. Simmer for about 5 minutes or until the sausages are halfway cooked. Remove the sausages from the liquid and set

them aside on a cutting board to cool. Save the cooking water for later use. Cut the sausages into 1-inch (2.5 cm) pieces.

3. In a skillet, heat oil over medium heat. Add the chicken thighs, skin side down, and brown them for about 5 minutes until nicely browned. Flip the chicken over and brown the other side as well. The chicken should be about three-quarters cooked through. Remove the chicken from the pan.

4. Add the leek, scallion greens, bell pepper, and celery to the same skillet. Sauté the vegetables for about 3 minutes, stirring often, until softened but not browned. Stir in the tomatoes and bay leaf, and then add the rice and 4 cups (960 ml) of the reserved sausage cooking water/stock. Top off with water to reach 4 cups (960 ml) if needed. Nestle the chicken pieces in the sauce, skin side up, and scatter the sausage pieces around them.

Cover the skillet, boil the mixture, then reduce the heat and cook for 20 to 30 mins until the rice is cooked and most liquid is absorbed. The jambalaya should have a juicy consistency. The Chicken & Sausage Jambalaya is now ready to be served. It can also be refrigerated in an airtight container for up to 3 days and reheated gently on the stovetop or microwave.

Quinoa Porridge with Berries and Cinnamon

Ingredients

- 1/4 tsp   ground cinnamon
- 4 tsp   pure maple syrup
- 10   raspberries (fresh or frozen)
- 20   blueberries (fresh or frozen)
- 1 tsp   neutral oil (rice bran, canola, sunflower)
- 250 ml (1 cup) water
- 188 ml (3/4 cup) low FODMAP milk

Instructions:

1. Measure the quinoa and rinse it under cold running water for two minutes using a fine mesh sieve. Transfer the rinsed quinoa to a

medium-sized saucepan and add a drizzle of neutral oil.

2. Toast the quinoa overheat for 1 to 2 minutes until the water evaporates and the quinoa is lightly toasted.
3. Add the water to the saucepan. Bring the quinoa to a rolling boil, then reduce the heat to the lowest setting. Cover the pan with a lid and allow the quinoa to cook for 12 to 15 minutes until it becomes fluffy.
4. If there is excess water, drain it and return the quinoa to the pan.
5. Add the low-FODMAP milk, cinnamon, and maple syrup to the pan. If the low FODMAP milk is absorbed completely, you can add more if desired. Allow the porridge to cook for about 5 minutes or till heated through. If you're using frozen berries and want them heated, add them to the mixture.

6. Serve the hot quinoa porridge in bowls and evenly divide the raspberries and blueberries between them.

Carrot Cake with Pecans (8 Servings)

Ingredients:

- 200g gluten-free self-rising flour
- 1 tsp cinnamon
- 1 tsp gluten-free baking powder
- 50g pecans, chopped
- For the icing
- 75g butter, softened
- 175g icing sugar
- 3 tsp cinnamon plus extra for dusting
- 140g unsalted butter, softened, plus extra for greasing
- 200g caster sugar
- 250g carrots, grated
- 140g sultanas

- 2 eggs, lightly beaten

Instructions:

1. Heat oven to 350F. Grease and line a 2 lb bread loaf pan with baking parchment.
2. Beat the butter and sugar with a mixer until soft and fluffy, then add the grated carrot and sultanas. Add the eggs into the mixing bowl one at a time, scraping and stirring after each addition.
3. Add the flour, cinnamon, baking powder and most of the chopped pecans and mix well. Pour the mix into the loaf tin, then bake for 50-55 mins or until a knife inserted in the middle comes out clean. Allow to cool in the pan for 15 mins, then remove from the pan and cool completely on a wire rack.
4. While the loaf cake is baking, make the icing. Let the butter come to room temperature, until it is soft. Whip the butter in a large bowl

until it has doubled in volume, add the icing sugar and cinnamon, and then beat until the icing is thick and creamy. When the cake is cool to the touch, spread the icing on top, then sprinkle with cinnamon in a decorative pattern and drizzle the remaining chopped nuts.

Cinnamon Rolls

Ingredients:

- 1 can refrigerated cinnamon rolls with icing

Instructions:

1. Place the cinnamon rolls into the air fryer basket.
2. Cook at 350°F for 8 minutes, or until golden brown and cooked through.
3. Drizzle the icing over the cinnamon rolls and serve.

Breakfast Pizza

Ingredients:

- 1/2 slices of bacon, cooked and crumbled
- 1/4 cup diced tomatoes 4 cup diced onions
- 1/4 cup diced green bell peppers
- 1 large pre-made pizza crust
- 1/2 cup pizza sauce
- 4 large eggs, scrambled
- 1/2 cup shredded cheddar cheese

Instructions:

1. Spread pizza sauce over the pre-made pizza crust.
2. Add scrambled eggs, shredded cheese, crumbled bacon, diced tomatoes, onions, and green bell peppers on top of the pizza sauce.
3. Place the pizza into the air fryer basket.

4. Cook at 350°F for 8-10 minutes, or until the crust is golden brown and crispy.

Easy Breakfast Sausage

Ingredients:

- ⅛ teaspoon red pepper flakes
- ⅛ teaspoon freshly ground black pepper
- Nonstick cooking spray
- 1 pound ground pork
- 1 teaspoon ground sage
- ½ teaspoon sea salt

Instructions:

1. In a large bowl, mix the pork, sage, salt, red pepper flakes, and pepper. Form the mixture into 8 patties.
2. Spray a large nonstick skillet with cooking spray and place it over medium-high heat.

3. Add the sausage patties and cook for about 4 minutes per side, until browned on both sides.

Orange-scented Overnight Oatmeal

Ingredients:

- 1 tablespoon maple syrup, divided
- ¼ teaspoon cinnamon
- ½ teaspoon vanilla extract
- ¼ teaspoon orange extract
- ⅛ teaspoon ground ginger
- 1 cup gluten-free rolled oats
- 1¼ cups lactose-free milk, divided
- Juice of ½ orange
- ½ tablespoon chia seeds

Instructions:

1. In a medium bowl, stir together the oats, 1 cup of the milk, orange juice, chia seeds, half of the maple syrup, cinnamon, vanilla and

orange extracts, and ginger. Cover and refrigerate overnight.
2. To serve, stir in the remaining maple syrup, and serve chilled or warmed.

Hawaiian Toasted Sandwich

Ingredients:

- 2 slices cheddar cheese
- 2 slices ham, cold cut
- 1 tbsp spring onion, tips finely chopped
- Pinch of black pepper
- 2 slices bread
- 1 tbsp butter
- 2 ½ tbsp pineapple chunks, drained

Instructions:

1. Place a frying pan over medium heat.
2. Spread butter on the outside of each slice of bread.

3. Prepare the filling by grating the cheese, slicing the ham, rinsing the pineapple, and chopping the spring onion finely.
4. Put the sandwich together adding pepper to taste and ensuring the butter is on the outside.
5. Place in the frying pan and cook each side for 3 minutes. The bread should turn golden brown. Serve warm.

Tomato And Green Bean Salad

Ingredients:

- Pinch of pepper
- 2 tbsp lactose-free or another FODMAP-approved milk
- 1 tbsp Dijon mustard
- 2 tomatoes
- 2 spring onions, green part only
- 1 ½ cups lettuce
- 1 cup green beans
- ½ cup mayonnaise
- ½ cup Greek yogurt
- 1 tbsp chopped basil
- 2 tbsp chopped parsley
- Pinch of salt

Instructions:

1. In a bowl, mix mayonnaise, yogurt, milk, mustard, basil, parsley, salt, and pepper.
2. Wash the green beans, lettuce, and spring onions, then drain the water and chop the green onions. Shred the lettuce into a separate bowl and mix in the green beans and spring onions.
3. Cut the tomatoes into quarters and mix into the bowl. Put the dressing into a serving jug and serve.

Maple–brown Sugar Oatmeal

Ingredients:

- 1 tablespoon unsalted butter
- 1 cup unsweetened almond milk
- ¼ cup packed brown sugar
- ¼ cup pure maple syrup
- Pinch sea salt
- 1 cup quick-cooking oatmeal (not instant)

Instructions:

1. In a medium saucepan over medium-high heat, heat the almond milk, brown sugar, maple syrup, butter, and salt until it simmers.
2. Stir in the oats. Bring to a boil, stirring frequently.
3. Reduce the heat to medium. Cover and simmer for 5 minutes, until the oatmeal thickens.

QUINOA BERRY BREAKFAST BAKE

Ingredients

- 1/4 cup walnuts chopped (or more)
- 3 eggs
- 3 cups lactose-free milk
- 1/4 cup maple syrup or brown sugar
- 1 tbsp cinnamon
- 1 tsp ginger
- 1 tsp butter/oil for greasing pan
- 1.5 cup quinoa dry/uncooked
- 1.5 cups strawberries
- 1 cup blueberries
- 1/2 cup raspberries

Instructions:

1. Preheat your oven to 375 degrees F.

2. Grease a large baking dish with butter or oil. Pour the quinoa into the dish and lightly shake to distribute the quinoa evenly.
3. Slice the strawberries. Sprinkle the berries and walnuts over the quinoa in the dish.
4. In a large bowl whisk the eggs. Stir the milk, syrup and spices into the eggs. Gently pour over the quinoa mixture.
5. Bake in preheated oven for 1 hour until the quinoa has absorbed all of the liquid. Extra servings can be kept in the fridge for up to 5 days or the freezer for months.

SCRAMBLED EGGS WITH SMOKED SALMON & CREAM CHEESE

Ingredients

- 2 tablespoons unsalted butter
- 8 ounces (225 g) cold-smoked salmon, torn or cut into bite-sized pieces, divided
- 4 ounces (115 g) lactose-free cream cheese, divided
- Fresh chives
- Fresh dill
- 12 large eggs, at room temperature
- Kosher salt
- Freshly ground black pepper

Instructions:

1. Whisk eggs very well in a large bowl with a splash of water and season well with salt and pepper; set aside.
2. Melt butter in a large, nonstick skillet until foamy over low-medium heat, swirling it around to coat the pan bottom and up the sides a little bit. Add the eggs and cook gently for a minute or two, then begin to bring the edges in towards the center as they begin to set. Dot the surface with half of the smoked salmon and half of the cream cheese and continue to scramble the eggs until they are light and fluffy, but still a tad moist and not dry.
3. Quickly dot the surface with remaining smoked salmon and cream cheese, add some snipped chives and fresh dill, to taste, and serve immediately.

QUINOA PORRIDGE WITH BERRIES AND CINNAMON

Ingredients

- 1/4 tsp ground cinnamon
- 4 tsp pure maple syrup
- 10 raspberries (fresh or frozen)
- 20 blueberries (fresh or frozen)
- 85 g (1/2 cup) quinoa
- 1 tsp neutral oil (rice bran, canola, sunflower)
- 250 ml (1 cup) water
- 188 ml (3/4 cup) low FODMAP milk

Instructions:

1. Measure out the quinoa. Using a fine mesh sieve rinse it under cold running water for two minutes. Transfer it to a medium sized saucepan and add a drizzle of neutral oil. Toast the quinoa over medium heat for 1 to 2 minutes until the water has evaporated and the quinoa is lightly toasted. Add the water. Bring the quinoa to a rolling boil and then turn down the element to the lowest heat setting. Cover with a pot lid and allow to cook for 12 to 15 minutes. The quinoa should be quite fluffy. Drain off any excess water if needed and return to pan.
2. Then add the low FODMAP milk, cinnamon, and maple syrup. If all the low FODMAP milk disappears you can add a little bit more. Then allow the porridge to simmer for about 5 minutes or until heated through. If you are using frozen berries and want them heated then add them to the mixture.

3. Serve the hot quinoa porridge into bowls and divide the raspberries and blueberries equally between them.

www.ingramcontent.com/pod-product-compliance
Lightning Source LLC
LaVergne TN
LVHW020436070526
838199LV00063B/4760